FREEDOM LIGHT

FREEDOM LIGHT

by
EDITH M. GAINES

ILLUSTRATIONS
by
CLIFF CLAY

NEW DAY PRESS   CLEVELAND, OHIO

PUBLISHED BY: New Day Press
Karamu House
2355 East 89th Street
Cleveland, Ohio 44106

New Day Press is a non-profit corporation established in 1972. It encourages minority group members to tell their own stories in their own way. It also strives to provide literature from which all children can learn the true story of American minorities.

New Day Press paperbacks are being used in schools and libraries across the United States and are distributed through Reading Is Fundamental (RIF), Inc., the national reading program.

The findings of this publication do not necessarily represent the view of the Ohio Humanities Council or the National Endowment for the Humanities.

Printed in the United States of America

Library of Congress Catalogue Number 91-060111

ISBN 0-913678-20-1

Table of Contents

Acknowledgments

Research Consultants:

Humanities Scholar Adrienne Lash Jones, Acting Chair, Department of Black Studies, Oberlin College

Humanities Scholar Allan Peskin, Professor of History, Cleveland State University

Also: Bonita Kirk, Eugene Settles, Miriam S. Zachman of Ripley, Ohio and Paul Young of Hillsboro, Ohio

Planning Committee:

Charles Castle, Superintendent of Schools, Ripley-Union-Lewis School District, Ripley, Ohio

Ebraska Ceasor, President, New Day Press

Ruth M. Hadlow, Children's Literature, Cleveland Public Library

Bonita Kirk, Ripley Heritage, Inc.

Lee Lassic, Editorial Committee, New Day Press

Rhonda McClanahan, Ripley Presbyterian Church

Benjamin Pedigo, Always A River Project, Ripley, Ohio

Bette Plymesser, Union Township Library, Ripley, Ohio

Delois Williams, Cleveland Public School Teacher

W. Hal Workman, Art Consultant, Cleveland, Ohio

Paul Young, Brown County Historian, Hillsboro, Ohio

This publication is made possible, in part, by the Ohio Humanities Council under a grant from the National Endowment for the Humanities. Support has also been received from TRW, Inc., Parker Hannifin Corporation, the Presbytery of Cincinnati, and the Ripley Presbyterian Church.

Introduction

Ripley, Ohio is an Ohio River town about fifty miles east of Cincinnati. In the 1820's the river was vital to the transportation of Ohio valley crops to market and for bringing manufactured goods to the river communities. At that time, the river boats had flat bottoms, designed especially for the shallow river, and some were powered by steam engines. Ripley, a small town of about 1500, had a thriving shipbuilding industry.

Because there were no bridges across the Ohio River in the 1820's, the river was a real barrier between Ohio and Kentucky except in the middle of winter when the ice was often thick enough for wagons to cross on it. For crossing the river, every little town had a ferry, a flat boat with two paddle wheels, big enough to carry vehicles as well as people. A horse was harnessed to each paddle wheel which turned as he walked—much like a treadmill. Many people, especially farmers, had their own small row boats or skiffs.

Since the Ohio River was also the dividing line between slave and free states, it always played an important part in the long history of the fight against slavery—a cruel institution that considered people as property, to be bought and sold as if they were horses. Owners had the legal right to mistreat slaves in the most brutal ways.

Whenever they could, slaves found ways to escape. The network of people, Black and White, who helped them became known as the Underground Railroad. Ripley was famous in the years before the Civil War for its Underground Railroad and other antislavery activities.

This book is the story of the antislavery heroes of Ripley, based on eyewitness accounts by two of their leaders—John Rankin, a Presbyterian minister whose grandfather came from Ireland; and John Parker, a businessman and inventor of African-American descent, who started life as a slave. There were many others who worked hard to end slavery and who participated as passengers or conductors in Ripley's Underground Railroad during the four-and-a-half decades from 1820 until the end of the Civil War in 1865. We are fortunate that these two men told their life stories so that we can see the Ripley story through their eyes.

Other sources of information for this book are *Ripley, Ohio, Its History and Families*, by Eliese B. Stivers and *Uncle Tom's Cabin* by Harriet Beecher Stowe. Unpublished information has been provided by Bonita Kirk, Eugene Settles, and Miriam S. Zachman of Ripley, Ohio, and Paul Young of Hillsboro, Ohio. The dialogue is written as it might have occurred.

As a tribute to the Rankins, the Ohio Historical Society and Ripley Heritage, Inc. operate the Rankin House as a state historical museum. The home of John Parker on Front Street is on the National Register of Historic Places. The people of Ripley erected a Liberty Monument which stands on the bank of the Ohio River at the foot of Ripley's Main Street. The names of John Rankin, John Parker and eleven other Ripley area men are carved on one side as a tribute to their work to end slavery.

Time Line

1787 Ordinance of 1787 outlawed slavery in the Northwest Territory, which included Ohio.

1793 John Rankin born in Tennessee.

1803 Ohio admitted to Union as a free state.

1822 John and Jean Rankin moved to Ripley and soon started Underground Railroad Activity.

1826 John Rankin's *Letters Against Slavery* published.

1827 John Percival Parker born in Norfolk, Virginia.

1835 John Rankin helped organize Ohio Antislavery Society.

1836 John Rankin spent a year lecturing for American Antislavery Society.

1850 Fugitive Slave Act passed.

1850 John Parker moved to Ripley and began working in Underground Railroad.

1854 John Parker opened Phoenix Foundry.

1861 Civil War began with attack on Fort Sumter.

1865 Slavery ended with passage of Thirteenth Amendment; Civil War ended.

Chapter 1

Words As Weapons
Against Slavery

"There's the river," John Rankin said as he pulled on the reins. The horse and carriage came to a stop at the top of a hill. The road ahead wound through the snow-tipped trees down to the Ohio River; a wide ribbon of ice glittering in the January sun. Across the river a cluster of buildings nestled in the shadow of the tree-covered hill on the Ohio side.

John pointed to the houses. "That's Ripley," he said to his children.

"That's going to be our new home!" five-year-old Adam exclaimed as Isabella and David clapped their hands excitedly.

"I know you and the children are glad we are almost there," John said to his wife, Jean, who was holding the baby, bundled to protect him from the cold.

Jean smiled. "The children can hardly wait," she said. "Can you see the church from here?"

"There it is!" John pointed to the steeple. "I will be preaching there on Sunday," the slender, boyish looking Rankin explained to his children.

It was January, 1822 and John Rankin was to be the pastor at the Ripley Presbyterian Church. Four years earlier John and Jean, with one child, had left their native Tennessee. They planned to move to Ohio because John was determined to preach against slavery and that was hard to do in a slave state like Tennessee. Jean had helped make that first move possible by persuading her father to give them a horse, a two wheeled carriage and seventy silver dollars.

1

Although they were bound for Ohio the first time, that trip had ended in Concord, Kentucky. John had been invited to be the pastor at a small Presbyterian church there. Kentucky was a slave state, but most of the Concord church members opposed slavery. However, public sentiment in Kentucky was becoming more pro-slavery. By the fourth year some of the families in the Concord church decided to move to free states. Since the congregation was small, it became increasingly difficult for John to support his growing family.

When the church in Ripley, Ohio and a second church, Strait Creek, a few miles away, needed a pastor, John was delighted to accept the call to serve both small churches. He knew there were people in Ripley who would help him with antislavery work.

The young preacher was welcomed in Ripley. His genuine interest in people won him many friends. Right away he started talking with other men in Ripley about organizing to put an end to slavery. Alexander Campbell, the Collins brothers, David Ammen and Thomas McCague were among the men who agreed to work with him. Women rarely spoke in public in those days, but Kitty McCague was a strong supporter of antislavery action and Jean Rankin was the first person John turned to for advice and encouragement.

When they first moved to Ripley, the Rankins built a large house on Front Street—just a stone's throw from the river. Although she was very busy getting settled in their new home, she became known as a person who always had time to help a sick neighbor or someone in need.

One day in December, 1823 John Rankin received a letter from his brother Thomas in Virginia. He frowned as he read it. "I can't believe that my own brother has purchased a slave," he said sorrowfully to Jean.

The next few days the young preacher spent a lot of time sitting, looking out the window at the ever-changing river and the wintry Kentucky hills. What could he tell his brother that might get him to change his mind?

"First I will tell him why I hate slavery," he thought and decided to write a letter. He picked up a quill pen and wrote, read the page over, shook his head and crumpled up the paper. He tore up the next sheet he wrote, but finally had a letter that said what he wanted. Even then Rankin was not satisfied that he had written enough to convince his brother, so he wrote a second letter, this one arguing that Blacks were created by the same God as Whites. The river was frozen solid and wagons were crossing on the ice by the time he finished that letter.

Rankin decided the evils of slavery needed to be written in detail, so his third letter listed some of what he had seen as an eyewitness to slavery during his years growing up in Tennessee and as a young preacher in Kentucky. He wrote:

"Thousands of slaves are pressed with the gnawings of hunger during their whole lives . . . When they return to their miserable huts at night, on the cold ground they must lie without covering, and shiver while they sleep . . . Many poor slaves are tortured with the lash . . . Thousands of whips are every day stained in African blood."

When Rankin finished that letter the river had an angry look. Big chunks of ice were tossed around by the rain-swollen waters. Still he was not sure that what he had written would cause his brother, or others who supported slavery, to change their minds.

Next, the young preacher thought about all the arguments against slavery he found in the Bible and decided to write those to his brother. Rankin wrote a total of thirteen letters. By the time the last letter was written, the river had the lazy look of summer.

Still uncertain about mailing the letters to his brother, John took them to his friend David Ammen. "What do you think of these?" he asked.

Ammen was so impressed he got permission to print all of them in his newspaper, *The Castigator*. Rankin then mailed the newspapers to his brother. Soon the letters began to be circulated widely in southern Ohio and Kentucky because no one had seen the case against slavery argued so eloquently. By 1826 they were printed in book form. In Maysville, Kentucky Bookseller Cox bought copies for his store, sold them all and bought some more. The letters found their way to the eastern states. In 1832 William Lloyd Garrison reprinted them in the second issue of his antislavery newspaper, *The Liberator.*

Writing the thirteen letters helped John Rankin make crucial decisions about what needed to be done.

"Jean," he said to his wife. "I must preach immediate emancipation for the slaves. The Federal government should purchase all the slaves and set them free." Jean nodded agreement as John continued, "I want to start visiting other churches and help them organize antislavery societies. But if I do, you'll be at home alone with the children a lot of the time." He put his arm around his wife's shoulders. She was expecting their sixth child in a few months and Adam, the oldest, was only eight.

"It's important for you to go," Jean replied. "We'll be all right. We have such good neighbors, and Adam and Isabella will help me with the little ones."

As Rankin visited churches throughout southwestern Ohio he found strong antislavery sentiment, especially among Presbyterians, Methodists and Quakers. But those in favor of slavery were also very vocal.

When John Rankin attended a convention at Putnam, Ohio in 1835 to form a state antislavery society, the large meeting was surrounded by a stone-throwing mob. When he and another speaker locked arms and started for the man's home, they were hit with rotten goose eggs. This was the first of many times that John Rankin spoke at meetings which were attacked by mobs. But he never stopped speaking and the number of people opposing slavery kept growing. By 1837 there were 213 local antislavery societies in Ohio.

Chapter 2

The Rankin House, an Underground Railroad Station

Ripley was the first stop in a free state for men and women running away from slavery. Alexander Campbell and others had helped fugitive slaves even before the Rankins moved to Ripley. It wasn't long before John and Jean Rankin made their house available for overnight stays, meals and other assistance to the fugitives. Since John was often away from home, Jean assumed much of the responsibility for this part of the antislavery work which came to be known as the Underground Railroad.

There is an old Ripley story about the origin of the term "Underground Railroad." A man named Tice Davids swam across the river to Ripley one night, his owner rowing right behind him, gun in hand. When Tice reached the shore, he saw a shadowy figure beckoning him toward a nearby lumberyard. Tice followed and both disappeared among the piles of lumber.

The slave owner reached the shore a few minutes later. He was sure he had seen the man climb on shore, but saw no sign of him on the street. He walked up and down the streets of Ripley, knocking on doors asking, "Have you seen a slave running this way?" He could not find anyone who admitted to having seen a runaway slave. Finally, he returned to his boat emptyhanded and exclaimed in frustration to a man standing outside the lumberyard, "I'd like to know where he went!"

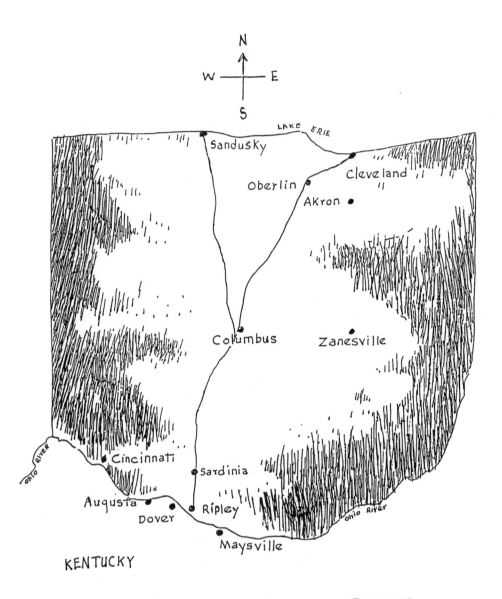

UNDERGROUND RAILROAD ROUTES

"Mister," the man said knowingly, "he must have taken an underground road." This joke was told all over Ripley and soon found its way clear to Sandusky where the first railroad tracks in Ohio were being laid. Before long, the expression became the "Underground Railroad."

As the number of escaping slaves increased, the Rankins decided that their house on Front Street was too close to the river to be a good "station" for their passengers. Slavehunters were often right on the heels of their escaping "property."

In 1828 the Rankins moved to a house on top of the bluff overlooking the river. What a move that must have been for a family that had grown to nine children—six sons and three daughters. Adam who was twelve, ten-year-old Isabella, nine-year-old David and Calvin, age seven, were all big enough to be a great deal of help to their mother and father. From the front windows of their new house, the Rankins could see almost six miles of the Ohio River and the Kentucky shoreline. Jean Rankin placed a light in the window every night—a light which could easily be seen from the Kentucky side. It came to be known as the Freedom Light.

When the Rankins moved to Liberty Hill, they left a number of co-workers down by the river, ready to greet escaping slaves and guide them to the steep path which led up the hill to the Rankin house. Among these guides were Dr. Alexander Campbell, Tom Collins, and a number of Black citizens—Rhoda Jones, Polly Jackson, Lindsey Jackson, Billy Martin, Joseph Settles and others whose names will never be known.

Ripley was just an overnight stop for most fugitives. Ohio's Black Laws, passed in 1804, made it illegal to give escaping slaves a place to stay or to interfere with their capture. A fugitive could not feel really safe anywhere in Ohio. John Rankin, as he traveled throughout southern Ohio, learned of others, both Black and White, who were willing to give aid to those fleeing from slavery. They, like the Rankins, obeyed what they believed were God's laws rather than unjust laws which had been made by men.

In the early years of this underground network, the first station after leaving Ripley was twenty-one miles north at Sardinia. Soon, however, the Presbyterian church at Red Oak, only four miles from Ripley, became a station.

As soon as the Rankin boys were old enough, they became "conductors," escorting passengers to the next underground station. Often that meant a trip at night on horseback. Sometimes it was a daytime trip, driving a wagon with passengers hidden under a load of hay or other crops from the farm. Adam or David would stop at the Red Oak church and deliver their passengers, then return home. The passengers would be escorted by conductors from one place to another until they reached Cleveland or Sandusky where they could board a boat for Canada. There they could be truly free.

Not long after the Rankins moved to Liberty Hill, the mood of proslavery Ohioans began to turn ugly. Their anger turned to violence. In 1829 there were three days of rioting in Cincinnati. The whole Black community of about 2200 was under attack—their homes burned, their lives in danger. Cincinnati remained so hostile that shortly afterward many of the Black families moved to Canada.

Ripley, only 50 miles from Cincinnati, felt shock waves from those riots. Many threats of violence were made against John Rankin. In 1838 Kentucky slaveholders offered $2500 for the assassination of John Rankin and Dr. Alexander Campbell. Rankin's sons and daughters kept watch each night at the house on Liberty Hill. One night his son Calvin heard a man whistle and saw him step behind the corner of the house. Calvin and a cousin each grabbed a pistol and ran out to search the premises. A shot rang out, grazing his shoulder and setting his shirt on fire. Calvin had to stop to put the fire out, so the man had escaped into the darkness by the time he could resume the pursuit. He and his cousin saw six men altogether and exchanged shots with them, chasing them off. The men had started a fire outside of one of the barns, but fortunately the night was damp and the fire went out. "The Lord preserved us all from harm," was John Rankin's comment.

This was only one of many attempts by armed men to ambush Rankin at his home. Such incidents made the work of aiding fugitives more difficult. However, the Rankin family was equal to the task and soon enlisted some of their neighbors to help. The Collins and Smith families nearby offered a place to sleep when the Rankin house and barns were full or when it was safer to stop someplace else. Others responded quickly to calls from one of the Rankin boys, "The slavehunters are on the hill!" More than once all the men poured out of the Black Wesleyan church at 3rd and Cherry and ran up the hill to surround the Rankin House.

One morning when John Rankin was away from home, Jean saw a strange man peering furtively around the corner of the barn. She stepped out on the porch to investigate. Putting her hand up to shield her eyes from the rays of the morning sun, Jean could make out the forms of several other men slinking out from among the trees in the peach orchard behind the barn. She could see their muskets glittering in the sun. Her three oldest sons—Adam, David, and Calvin—had gone down the hill to Ripley, so she called the next oldest, Samuel, to run down and find any of their friends who could come right away. She heard the front door slam and knew that he was on his way.

The men continued to move cautiously toward the house as Jean Rankin stood on the porch, her small figure silhouetted by the morning sun. Finally one of the men cupped his hands around his mouth and called to her.

"We're looking for a man, Miz Rankin. He broke in a store at Dover and came across the river in a skiff he stole. We followed him here so he must be hiding. Is he in your house?"

9

Jean's voice was calm as she called back, "Is the man White or Black?"

"It's a slave we've come for," the man shouted back.

Before Jean could reply, her son John burst out of the house and brushed by her, carrying his father's heavy musket. Standing on the edge of the porch, he aimed the gun right at the man standing by the barn.

"No slave hunter's coming in my house," the boy shouted.

The man turned to his companion. Jean could see their gestures and nodding of heads. Then he called again, "We're all armed. We'll search your house with or without your say so."

Just then, a young man stepped into the sun at the other end of the barn. It was one of the Rankin boys who had gone down the hill. Holding his musket in the crook of his arm, he shouted to the man, "I'd stay just about right where you are now."

Behind him appeared about a dozen other men and boys carrying revolvers, squirrel rifles or muskets. They moved closer to the intruders at the other side of the barn.

"You ought to be ashamed of yourselves, picking on a helpless woman and her children," one of the Ripley men said sternly to the slaveowners.

Meanwhile, another man joined the slaveowners to report that he had tried to get a search warrant from the Ripley magistrate, but had been refused. Again there was much gesturing in the little group. They were outnumbered two to one so they turned around and left. Not a shot had been fired. One more threat to the Rankins and their Underground Railroad station had been met with the help of their Ripley friends.

This incident was reported in the Ripley newspaper and the sentiments of the town's abolitionists were expressed by one letter to the editor: "I would remind my friends from across the river that if they murder Mr. Rankin, destroy his property, or even burn the town of Ripley, they will never save one slave by it . . . God

10

has given us the right of hospitality and we will never surrender it but with our lives."

Not everyone in Ripley agreed with these strong sentiments. There were many citizens who believed in upholding the Black Laws, however unjust they were. There were some who secretly aided the slaveowners any way they could. But with an antislavery society of over 300 members, the friendly atmosphere in Ripley made it possible for the Underground Railroad operators to continue escorting slaves on the long, dangerous route to freedom.

Chapter 3

John Parker and His Passengers

Often the fugitives who came across the Ohio River were afraid of strange White people. Their slave owners, to discourage them from running away, told false stories about abolitionists. Consequently, the Black citizens of Ripley and neighboring communities played a key role because the fugitives were more apt to trust them. However, very little has been written about Blacks who assisted escaping slaves. One of these unsung heroes was Joseph Settles, whose story is told by his grandson, Eugene. Brought up as a slave in Maysville, Kentucky, young Joseph was determined to seek freedom across the Ohio River. His mother was the housekeeper for the slave owner and Joseph was allowed to travel freely to Ripley and other nearby towns in Ohio. He learned that there were safe houses in and around Ripley where help was available for those escaping from slavery. Over a period of time, Joseph recruited twelve people willing to take the risks of going with him. He obtained a skiff and set a night for the escape. Joseph rowed across the river with six passengers, then returned for the other six. All twelve became passengers on the Underground Railroad. Joseph Settles was able to obtain his freedom, though his grandson does not know the details, and settled in Ripley, continuing to assist fugitives whenever he could.

Best known of the Black Underground Railroad operators in Ripley was John Parker who moved to Ripley in 1850. His daring soon increased the number of passengers passing through Ripley. Much later, he told the story of his early years and why he decided to risk his life helping slaves escape.

When the Rankins moved from Front Street to the house on Liberty Hill, John Parker was a baby in his mother's arms in Norfolk, Virginia. He never knew his father, a slave owner who permitted him to be sold away from his mother when he was eight years old.

The frightened boy was chained to an old man who he remembered trying to comfort him. As they walked—one hundred slaves altogether—the old man took as much of the weight of the chain as he could. Then, for no apparent reason, one of the slave drivers started whipping the old man and yelling at him to go faster. The old man stumbled and the driver whipped him again and again. Finally, he fell and did not get up again. The driver impatiently yanked the chains off the unconscious man and kicked his body off the road. The ninety-nine marchers went on, exhorted by the cruel drivers, and the old man was left to die.

John Parker never forgot the old man who befriended him when he was frightened and lonesome for his mother. He was more scared than ever with his friend gone. The fear gave way to anger when the driver whipped him. John picked up the first stick he saw and began striking at flowers, bubbles in the stream, anything that was free and unchained. It wasn't fair! He even tried to hit a redbird because it reminded him of the red blood streaming down the old man's back.

Many years later John Parker recalled that scene so vividly etched in his memory and said it was the beginning of his resolve to help slaves escape to freedom.

Meanwhile, the eight-year-old John was sold to a doctor in Mobile, Alabama and grew up as a houseboy. He had many privileges he would not have had if he had worked in the fields. The doctor's two sons taught him to read and write. When his work was finished, he would take the Bible or books of Shakespeare to the hay loft and read.

His years as a houseboy came to an end when the

doctor's sons went off to college and John was apprenticed, first to a plasterer and then to a foundry where he learned iron moulding, work that he liked and learned quickly. The doctor sold John to a woman in Birmingham, Mrs. Ryder. This turned out to be a fortunate change in masters for the young man because Mrs. Ryder agreed to let him keep the money he earned at the foundry. In less than two years he had saved $1800 and purchased his freedom.

Young John Parker immediately headed north, resolving to find a way to help those he was leaving behind. They were being treated like animals, he said to himself. The beatings they suffered were bad, but he felt the worst thing of all was the degradation of not being allowed to think for themselves or decide what to do with their lives.

In Cincinnati John met a free man, a barber, who convinced him to go with him to Maysville, Kentucky and rescue two girls who wanted to escape slavery by going north. Just a few miles west of Maysville, on the other side of the river was Ripley. John had heard about the Rankins and their antislavery work. That might be just the place for him to settle. With his iron-working skills he soon found work.

By this time there was heavy traffic on the Underground Railroad. When the water was low in the summer some waded across. In midwinter they walked across on the ice. Some were lucky enough to get a ride in a small row boat or skiff.

John Parker soon bought a small boat and started rowing across to Kentucky at night after finishing work. He had a wife and small children to feed, but still was able to save money and open his own business, the Phoenix Foundry, in 1854.

As foundry owner, John Parker had more freedom for his Underground Railroad operations. When he talked to the men and women that he rowed across the river, Parker learned that there were many others who would come if they had a guide to lead them to the river. He began to make longer and more frequent trips into Kentucky to lead groups of fugitives to the river. Each time he made arrangements with another Underground operator to meet him with a boat when he returned to the river with his party.

Once he saw a poster, "Reward $1000 for John Parker, dead or alive"—not a sight to quiet his nerves, he admitted. But, like John Rankin, he kept right on with his work. No one was going to intimidate him.

However, Parker did find it necessary to take precautions. The big man made it a habit to walk down the middle of the street, looking right and left so he would not be ambushed from a dark alley. He had to be wary even of those he wanted to help. One time a Black man from Kentucky knocked on his door saying that he was trying to escape from his master. Something about his manner made Parker suspicious that he was acting as a decoy for the slave hunters. John Parker jerked the man inside and closed the door.

"We must hurry if you want to be free," Parker said and rushed the man out the back way and over to Tom Collins' house. He told Collins to get the man to the next station as quickly as possible. That was one man who was literally hijacked to freedom against his wishes. When Parker returned home and slave catchers appeared at his door, the man was nowhere to be seen and Parker had fooled them again.

Slave catchers often came right into Ripley in pursuit of the escaping property. One time Parker was leading two runaways to a safe house when he caught sight of the slave owner. They were close to Tom Collins' undertaking parlor, so Parker ran in, followed by the two men. Collins quickly found three empty coffins and the men jumped in. A few minutes later the slave owner appeared, swearing he had seen his men running down that very street.

"Nobody here but me and the corpses," Collins assured him. Seeing nothing but coffins, the frustrated slaveowner went away. Parker and Collins had a good laugh about that escape.

Sometimes John Parker was almost foolhardy. A White moulder from Kentucky named Jim Shrofe worked in Parker's foundry. When he found out about his employer's slave rescue trips, he dared him to try getting away with any of his father's slaves. Maybe he was scheming to get the $1000 reward offered for Parker in Kentucky. Nevertheless, Parker accepted the challenge and made several secret trips to the Shrofe slave quarters to find who would like to go north. He found a young couple eager to make the trip, but they were worried about how to get their baby out. In order to keep them from running away, their master had their baby sleep at the foot of his bed where he kept a lighted candle and a loaded pistol.

Determined to overcome this obstacle, Parker had the couple describe the inside of the house. He chose a night that Jim Shrofe had taken the dogs to go coon hunting. Parker took off his shoes, crawled into the bedroom and picked up the baby. Then he threw the baby's pillow knocking the candle and the loaded pistol off the table. The sound wakened the elder Shrofe, but he couldn't see what was happening. Before he found a light, Parker, the baby and the couple were running toward the boat waiting for them at the river. They were about halfway across the river when shots rang out—shots intended for them. Parker told his passengers to lie down in the boat and he rowed as hard as he could. He was able to get his passengers safely passed on to another Underground operator before Shrofe's father got across the river. Jim Shrofe never came back to work at the foundry.

At one time, Parker had a notebook with all the names of his passengers and the dates that he ferried them to safety. However, he burned the notebook for safety reasons and had only his memory as a record.

Chapter 4

More Passengers (Remembered by John Rankin)

The passengers on the Underground Railroad took many risks and displayed great courage during their long journeys from slave states to Canada where they were truly free. Since they had to travel in secret, most of their stories will never be known, but here are some that were told by John Rankin.

One story that he recalled was about a man and his wife from Dover, Kentucky who decided to go to Canada. First the husband left and after he got there safely, his wife started out, carrying their baby in her arms. After staying all night with one of the Rankins' neighbors, she continued her trip to Canada. The couple had left their other six children behind in Kentucky. Four years later the wife returned on foot to the Rankin House, saying that she planned to go to Kentucky to rescue her six children. John Rankin told her it would be a very dangerous trip, but she insisted on going. Rankin advised her to wear men's clothing as a disguise, which she did. Once in Kentucky, she hid all day in the shrubbery of her former master's garden and at night got four of her children and a grandchild. She was unable to rescue the two youngest children who slept in the master's house. The woman and the five children hid all the next day in a cornfield waiting for a chance to get back across the river. The second night, a Canadian brought them safely across the river and to the Rankin house. They all reached Canada safely.

One of the saddest stories John Rankin told was about a man who escaped from a plantation in Kentucky, more than a hundred miles south of the Ohio River. He succeeded in getting all the way to Canada—and freedom.

Since his wife and two children were still slaves in Kentucky, he was determined to go back for them. It wasn't too hard for him to get back to Ripley, but from Ripley across the river and south to the plantation was a very dangerous trip. The young man, inspired by his love for his family, faced those dangers without a thought for his own safety. He knew the route through Kentucky very well so he traveled through the dense woods whenever possible until he got to his master's plantation. He waited until night, then approached the slave quarters and got word to his wife. She dressed the two children and all four of them started toward the Ohio River.

As soon as the plantation owner discovered that the woman and two children were missing, he sent a slave catcher after them. The fleeing family, hurrying as fast as they could on foot, soon realized that they were being followed. One of the children just couldn't keep up. He was just far enough behind that the slave catcher was able to grab him. His parents had to rush on or they would have been caught too. Now it was three escaping to freedom.

They found a way to get across the Ohio River and to Ripley where they rested at the home of a Black family. However, after they left Ripley they had gone only a short distance when the slave catcher found them and pretended to be a friend. Before they realized what had happened, the slave catcher had put handcuffs on the man. His wife and children were returned to the Kentucky plantation. As for the man who loved his family so much that he risked his life to return for them, he was sent into hopeless slavery farther south. That was a common punishment for slaves who ran away. John Rankin was especially indignant about this because Ohio officials cooperated with the slave catcher in tearing this family apart and punishing the man for his courageous attempt to free his family.

Sometimes escaping slaves got help from sympathetic citizens of Augusta or Maysville, the closest towns to Ripley on the Kentucky side. John Rankin told about a slave woman in Augusta, a member of the Presbyterian church there, who was highly esteemed in the town. She helped her masters raise their children and they let her live as a free woman, but when they died, their heirs decided to sell her. The people of Augusta hid her until a free Black woman from Ohio rowed across the river and took her to the Rankin house.

Another story Rankin told was of a man in Maysville who hired a young slave woman to wait on his sick wife. While she was working there, her owner sold her and a slave driver came for her. The man refused to let her go, saying he had an agreement for her to work and that her time was not up. When the slave driver was gone, he told the young woman, "You are sold and I cannot help you. If you have any desire to go to Canada, now is your time." With that encouragement, the young woman left, crossed the river and after a brief stay at the Rankin House, went on to Canada.

While many of the Ripley Underground Railroad passengers were from Kentucky, there were also those who came from farther south, having made the long, treacherous journey by foot, hiding in woods and swamps until they reached the Ohio River. Rankin told of one man who had traveled so far that his shoes were worn out and his clothing in tatters. He stopped at a farmer's house near Ripley and asked if he could do some work. The farmer was quite prejudiced, but he needed help so he agreed. The man proved to be a good worker and changed the farmer's mind about Blacks. When the Black man felt he could trust the farmer, he told him he was a fugitive slave. The farmer hated to lose a good farm hand, but he knew that it wouldn't be safe for him to stay there indefinitely. So the farmer went to Goshen and told the abolitionists there that he had a fugitive slave who needed shoes, clothing and money to get to Canada. All these were soon collected and the man was on his way.

Often escaping slaves and those helping them risked their lives. John Rankin told of a woman owned by a Kentucky preacher who refused to let her join her free husband in Ripley. Her husband's brother, named Penny, took a friend and went to Kentucky to get her. When the preacher discovered the woman was gone, he hired two of his neighbors to get her back. They reached the ferry opposite Ripley before the woman they were pursuing; so they hid and waited. When Penny and his sister-in-law arrived, one of the pursuers pointed a pistol at him, demanding his surrender. Penny drew his pistol and said, "I can shoot as well as you can, I shall not surrender."

Penny grabbed the ferry boat so his sister-in-law and the man helping him could get on board. A fight ensued with Penny and his helper knocking one man down, then boarding the ferry. When the boat pulled away from the shore, the pursuers started shooting and Penny returned the fire, hitting one of the men. Penny, his sister-in-law and his helper, all reached the Ohio shore safely. Rankin himself saw the ferry man the next day— the man Penny had knocked down. His face was badly bruised and he told Rankin he had slipped and fallen from the river bank. As for the man who was shot, two antislavery doctors took care of him. Penny's wife stayed with a family in Ripley for a few days and then her husband was able to get her to a safe place.

Although John Rankin told some sad stories about fugitive slaves who were caught trying to escape, he said that no passenger who reached the Rankin House had ever been caught.

Chapter 5

Eliza, The Most
Famous Passenger

The most famous passenger on the Ripley Underground Railroad was Eliza, immortalized in the novel, *Uncle Tom's Cabin*, by Harriet Beecher Stowe. In 1852, the year the book was published, 300,000 copies were sold. This brought the antislavery message into the homes of many Americans. Mrs. Stowe had visited Ripley before writing her book and the story of Eliza bears marked similarities to actual events described by John Rankin.

As Mrs. Stowe tells the story, Eliza and her young son, Harry, were slaves on the Kentucky plantation of Mr. Shelby. The Shelbys treated their slaves fairly well, and Mrs. Shelby was personally opposed to slavery. Eliza's husband, George, on the other hand, belonged to a tyrannical master who made him do the hardest, most menial jobs on the farm. One evening George came to visit Eliza, bringing disturbing news.

"Master says he won't let me come back here anymore and that I must take Mina for a wife and settle down with her or he'll sell me down the river."

"But you're married to me by the minister, as much as if you'd been a White man," protested Eliza.

"Don't you know a slave can't be married? There's no law in this country for that. I can't keep you as my wife if my master says, "No," replied George bitterly. "So Eliza, my love, bear up now and goodbye for I'm going."

"Going, George! Going where?"

"To Canada," he said. "And when I get there I'll buy you and Harry—God helping me, I will!"

"But if you're caught?"

"I won't be caught, Eliza. I'll die first! I'll be free or I'll die!"

Eliza urged George to be careful, and gave him a tearful embrace. Her troubles were only beginning, for that very evening she overheard Mr. Shelby agree to sell her five-year-old son, Harry, to a slave trader. Then, hiding in a closet, she heard Mrs. Shelby try unsuccessfully to change her husband's mind. He had to do it, he said, because of debts.

Eliza tiptoed back to her room, hastily packed Harry's clothes into a bundle which she tied around her waist. Then she shook the little boy and dressed him. Harry looked at his mother who was wearing her bonnet and shawl.

"Where are you going, Mother?" he asked.

"Hush, Harry," said Eliza softly, "A wicked man was coming to take you away. But I won't let him. I'm going to run away with you."

Eliza glided noiselessly out of her room onto the veranda, carrying Harry in her arms. She stopped to tap on the window of Uncle Tom's cabin to tell him and Aunt Chloe what had happened. Then she disappeared into the darkness.

The next morning when the Shelbys and the other servants discovered that Eliza was gone there was a lot of excitement. Mrs Shelby said, "The Lord be thanked."

Mr. Shelby offered his two men and horses to Haley, the slave trader, to help him hunt for little Harry. "But do eat some breakfast first," he urged.

Mrs. Shelby gave directions to the servants which gave them the distinct impression that they should work very slowly. Aunt Chloe took twice as long as usual to prepare breakfast. Sam, who was in charge of the horses, slipped a small beechnut under the saddle of Haley's horse, so that the slightest weight on the saddle would hurt him.

After breakfast, Haley appeared on the veranda, ready to go. "Well, boys, we must lose no time!"

Sam brought the horse to Haley and handed him the reins. The instant Haley touched the saddle, the horse jumped nervously, threw his master sprawling to the ground, and pranced away across the lawn. Mysteriously, the other two horses were loose, also.

Haley ran up and down cursing and stamping his feet. Sam and Andy seemed to have a hard time catching the horses. At last, about noon, Sam appeared riding one of the horses with Haley's horse by his side. Both were reeking with sweat.

"You've lost me near three hours with your cursed nonsense," Haley said impatiently. "Now let's be off."

"Master," Sam explained quietly, "The horses are tired. We need to rub them down. Master shouldn't think of starting till after dinner."

It was two o'clock when the three men finally left the plantation. They got lost on the way, thanks to Sam's confusing directions.

As a result of all Haley's delays, Eliza was able to reach a small village by the Ohio River before her pursuers. She looked at the river and saw great cakes of floating ice piled up against each other with the rain-swollen water swirling around them. The ice cakes filled up the river, extending almost to the Ohio shore. Eliza saw that the ice might prevent the ferry boat from crossing the river, so she stopped at a small tavern to inquire.

"No indeed!" said the woman in the tavern. "The boats has stopped running."

"I've walked quite a piece today in hopes to get to the ferry," Eliza said; and her look of dismay aroused the woman's motherly sympathies.

"Solomon," the woman called. A man appeared at the door. "I say, is that man going to tote them barrels over tonight?"

"He said he'd try," replied the man.

The woman turned to Eliza and said, "You'd better sit down and wait."

Little Harry was crying, so the woman opened the door to a small bedroom and said to Eliza, "Let him rest in here." Eliza thanked her and Harry was soon fast asleep.

About three quarters of an hour after Harry fell asleep, Haley, Sam, and Andy came riding by the window where Eliza stood looking out. Sam's quick eye caught a glimpse of her. He dropped his hat and shouted to his horse to stop.

Eliza, hearing him, stepped away from the window. She hastily picked up the sleeping Harry and ran out the side door and down to the river. Haley caught a glimpse of her just as she disappeared down the bank. He jumped off his horse, called loudly to Sam and Andy to follow, and was after Eliza like a hound after a deer.

As Eliza reached the water's edge she found the strength God gives only to the desperate and made a flying leap, landing on an ice cake which pitched and creaked with her weight. With wild cries and desperate energy she leaped to another and still another ice cake—stumbling, slipping, but never loosening her grip on her sleeping child. Her shoes were gone, her stockings cut from her feet so that blood marked every step. But she kept on until she saw the Ohio side and a man with his hands stretched out to help her up the bank.

"You're a brave girl, whoever you are," said the man.

Eliza recognized the face of the man who owned a farm not far from her old house.

"Mr. Symmes—do hide me! My child's been sold to that trader," begged Eliza, pointing to the Kentucky shore.

"There's nowhere I could take you," he said kindly, then pointed to a large white house on a hill above the village. "Go there. They are kind folks and they'll help you."

"The Lord bless you," said Eliza earnestly. Then she walked swiftly toward the white house, carrying the sleeping Harry.

Other chapters of the novel described George's escape to Ohio, the eventual reunion of Eliza and Harry with George and their safe arrival in Canada.

Chapter 6

Triumph Over Slavery

When the Fugitive Slave Act was passed in 1850, the conflict between proslavery and antislavery forces became more heated. Many people came to feel, as John Parker and John Rankin did, that it should be disobeyed. Crowds of people rescued fugitives from courtrooms in Massachusetts, New York, Wisconsin, and Ohio. The war of words was heating up, too—in Congress, in the newspapers, on the streets.

In 1852 *Uncle Tom's Cabin* was published and the book did more than all the antislavery speeches had done to convince people in the North to oppose slavery.

As John Rankin read the newspapers, he began to have forebodings. "Jean," he said to his wife, "Slavery will be ended in our lifetime. I'm sure of that—but I'm afraid the end won't come peacefully."

John Parker read about the State Convention of Ohio Colored Men held in 1858 and the speeches made in Cincinnati by Black antislavery lecturer, Frances E. Harper, denouncing the government. He also felt that war was coming.

Both men were even more convinced that there would be a war between the North and the South when John Brown and a small band of men attacked Harper's Ferry on October 16, 1859. In fact, all Ripley citizens began to steel themselves for war.

Ripley voters went to the polls in November, 1860 and helped elect Abraham Lincoln as President, knowing that he was against slavery, but that his strongest conviction was to save the United States from being torn apart. Yet, even before Lincoln took office, the country moved closer and closer to Civil War. By the time President Lincoln was inaugurated, seven southern states had seceded from the Union.

When the news came on April 12, 1861 that Confederate soldiers had attacked Fort Sumter, the men of Ripley held a meeting at the Methodist church and started recruiting for the Union army. The Confederates pledged to "burn that abolitionist hell-hole, Ripley, to the ground." Ripley citizens were determined to keep that from happening. All the men too old or too young for the army formed a Home Guard which was often called out. Sometimes these exciting episodes began with a series of lantern flashes from the Kentucky hills. The bells of the churches sounded the alarm. From every house the boys and the old men would rush out with their guns in their hands. Sometimes it was a false alarm. Sometimes there were shots exchanged, but Ripley was never attacked.

Kentucky stayed with the Union and Ripley's Home Guard responded to more than one call for assistance from their sister towns across the river—Augusta and Maysville.

In July, 1863 Confederate Raider John Morgan and his troops marched along the Ohio River. The Ripley Home Guard notched trees along the way so they could be quickly thrown across the road if needed to stop the raiders. Several companies of Union men, including a detachment of Black volunteers, fought off Morgan until he was captured. Ripley was saved again.

Five of John Rankin's sons and one grandson joined the Union forces. As soon as the Union army accepted Black soldiers, John Parker recruited an entire regiment, most of them men from Kentucky. Both John Parker and John Rankin rejoiced when the Civil War was over and slavery in the United States was finally ended with the passage of the Thirteenth Amendment.

As he looked back on the lifelong struggle which he had begun as a student in Tennessee, John Rankin said, "I lived to see four million slaves freed, but not in the peaceful way I worked to have it done. I wanted the government to pay the owners and then set all the slaves free. Four thousand million dollars in property and money could have been saved if my plan had been followed, and what is more important, more than half a million lives could have been saved from a bloody death."

John Parker, who had dedicated his life to ending slavery when he was a child chained to one hundred other slaves, also looked back on the years of the anti-slavery movement and said, "I can say that Ripley wielded more influence than any other town, big or little. It was the real terminus of the Underground Railroad."

John Parker's words were a tribute to the many citizens of Ripley who helped keep the Freedom Light burning, not only in the window of the Rankin House, but also in the hearts of those struggling to end slavery. The bravest of all these were the Underground Railroad passengers. John and Jean Rankin and their children, John Parker and the other Underground Railroad conductors and stationmasters, and all the passengers deserve our thanks for their contributions to freedom.

Biographical Notes

John and Jean Rankin

John Rankin was born February 4, 1793 in Jefferson County, Tennessee, one of twelve children of Richard Rankin, a farmer and blacksmith. At the age of 17 John entered Washington College, Jonesborough, Tennessee and graduated in 1814.

The same year he married Jean Lowry (born December 1, 1795). The couple had nine sons and three daughters. They also adopted and raised a niece.

John Rankin was licensed to preach in 1816 and served as a Presbyterian minister throughout his active years. He was pastor of the Presbyterian Church in Ripley from 1822 to 1845 when the church split over antislavery issues. Rankin's followers set up the Free Presbyterian Church and he continued as pastor of that congregation until 1866 when both ministers resigned and the two churches were reunited. After that, John Rankin preached for a number of years in Central Illinois and in Kansas.

Jean Rankin died in 1877 after 63 years of marriage. John Rankin died in 1886 at Ironton, Ohio at the age of 93. Both are buried in Ripley's Maplewood Cemetery.

John P. Parker

John Percival Parker was born in Norfolk, Virginia in 1827. In 1845 he purchased his freedom for $1800 from Mrs. Ryden of Mobile, Alabama.

He married Miranda Boulden of Cincinnati on May 12, 1848. Seven children were born to the couple.

In 1850 John Parker and his family moved to Ripley. In 1854 he opened the Phoenix Foundry on Front Street. Later he built a machine shop next to the foundry. The business flourished and was generally considered important to Ripley's prosperity in the 1870's and '80's. At one time Parker had at least 25 employees.

John P. Parker also patented several inventions, including a follower screw for tobacco presses (1884), a portable screw press (1885), and a soil pulverizer (1890).

Little has been recorded about John Parker's personal life or his family. In 1883, three of his sons were reported to be school teachers.

John P. Parker died in Ripley in 1900 and was buried in Maplewood Cemetery.

Glossary

Abolitionist. A person who wanted to end slavery. Abolitionists organized the Underground Railroad.

Antislavery. Opposed to one human being owning another. Many people worked to abolish the practice of slavery.

Assassination. Murder—especially of a high-level, powerful person. President Abraham Lincoln was assassinated.

Civil War. The 1861–1865 battle between the North and South that forced the South back into the Union of American states. This conflict, plus the Thirteenth Amendment to the Constitution, ended slavery.

Confederate Army. The army of the Southern states during the Civil War that fought the Union Army.

Ferry. A flat boat with 2 paddle wheels, big enough to carry vehicles as well as people. Ferries were used to cross the Ohio River.

Foundry. A business establishment that melts metal by heat for pouring into molds of various shapes. John Parker, a former slave, opened a foundry.

Fugitive. A runaway. Many slaves fled their captors.

Inaugurate. To introduce into public use by some formal ceremony to announce the event. Abraham Lincoln was sworn into the office of President of the United States.

Lecturer. A person who speaks on a subject (usually before a group of people) to inform others. John Rankin spoke frequently to groups to garner support to end slavery.

Magistrate. A person responsible for administering the law—especially for minor crimes.

Methodist. One of the largest denominations of the Protestant religion. Many members opposed slavery.

Musket. A handgun for infantry soldiers (predecessor of

the rifle). This firearm, six- to seven-feet long, was used by both sides in the Civil War.

Plantation. A large farm or estate where laborers (usually residents) grow tobacco, cotton, and other products in large quantities. Most slaves lived on and worked this acreage.

Presbyterian. One of the largest denominations of the Protestant religion. John Rankin, a Presbyterian, lost his ministry because of his abolitionist activities.

Proslavery. In favor of the continuance of human bondage; either because it wasn't considered wrong, or because of sympathy with the South's economic dependency on slave labor.

Quaker. One of the smallest denominations of the Protestant religion, and was noted for opposition to war and slavery.

Quill Pen. A writing instrument fashioned from the hard, tubelike part of a feather.

Secede. Withdraw from an alliance—such as the South breaking away from the Union of American states.

Skiff. A boat small enough for sailing or rowing by one person. Many people sailed the Ohio River in their own boats.

Union Army. Northern army during the Civil War that forced the South back into the Union of states.

Underground Railroad. The secret network of people and places that helped runaway slaves escape.

Veranda. A porch (walkway or seating area) attached to the outside of a house.

Additional Reading

References for Young Readers

Blockson, Charles L., "The Underground Railroad."
  National Geographic, July 1984, pp. 3–39
Hamilton, Virginia, *The People Could Fly*. Alfred Knopf,
  1985, pp. 141–146
Havighurst, Walter, *River to The West*. G. P. Putnam's
  Sons, 1970, Chapter 20
Rosebloom, Eugene & F. Weisenberger, *A History of
  Ohio*. The Ohio Historical Society, 1967
Stein, R. Conrad, *Story of The Underground Railroad*.
  Children's Press, 1981
Stowe, Harriet Beecher, *Uncle Tom's Cabin*, 1966 adap-
  tation by Anne Terry White, George Braziller, Inc.

References for Adults

Blockson, Charles L., *The Underground Railroad*. Pren-
  tice Hall, 1987
Gregg, Frank, *Autobiography of John Parker*. Unpub-
  lished manuscript, Duke University Library
Filler, Louis, *Crusade Against Slavery*. Reference Pub-
  lications, Inc., 1986 edition
Rankin, John, *Life of Rev. John Rankin Written by
  Himself in His Eightieth Year*, Unpublished Manu-
  script, Union Township Library, Ripley, OH.
Ripley Heritage, Inc., *Ripley, Ohio, Its History and Fam-
  ilies*, 1965
Siebert, Wilbur H., *Mysteries of Ohio's Underground
  Railroad*. Long's College Book Co., Columbus, OH,
  1951
Young, Paul, "John Parker: Ripley's Black Abolition-
  ist" in *Ohio Southland*, Winter, 1990

About the Artist
Cliff Clay

Cliff Clay is a nationally known artist and old west historian; and is also a sculptor and inventor. Inspiration for his illustrations was gained from first-hand experience with customs, culture and heritage of others by living and working on ranches and reservations throughout the fourteen major western states, the Canadian West, and Mexico.

His art work has been widely presented through slides, lectures, workshops, art exhibits; with special presentations to schools, colleges, and universities. With the support of the South Carolina Arts Commission and the National Endowment of the Arts, Cliff Clay painted the "Back Down Home Series,"—four drawings from this series appear in another New Day Press book, "Fireside Tales."

About the Author
Edith M. Gaines

Edith M. Gaines, one of the Founders of New Day Press publishing company in 1972, is currently Vice President for Advertising and Promotion for the company. Currently retired (except for many community activities), she was an Assistant Professor of Early Childhood Education at St. John's College in Cleveland, Ohio; and was employed as an Early Childhood Specialist for the Council for Economic Opportunities. She also gave extensive assistance to the development of the Head Start program in Cleveland, Ohio.

Published works by Edith include stories in New Day Press's Black History Series I and II, and Black Image Makers; and stories published in children's magazines: Ranger Rick; Jack and Jill; and Highlights for Children.

Her interest in the historical events that occurred along the Ohio River (especially in Ripley, Ohio), was sparked in 1979 when she accompanied a group of children to Ripley as part of the Summer Program for Children in Cleveland, Ohio. Guided by members of the Ripley Presbyterian Church, they toured the historical Underground Railroad sites—the homes of John Rankin and John Parker, a monument to them, the Ohio River, and other historical sites in the city.

The children's interest and enthusiasm about the stories told to them by the guides, and Edith's own fondness for American history, compelled her to search out more detail to help preserve this major chapter of American history.